America

A VIEW FROM ABOVE

Captions: Fleur Robertson
Design: Philip Clucas MSIAD
CLB 2458
© 1989 Colour Library Books Ltd, Godalming, Surrey, England.
All rights reserved.
This 1989 edition published by Portland House, a division of dilithium Press, Ltd,
distributed by Crown Publishers, Inc, 225 Park Avenue South, New York, New York 10003.
Printed and bound in Spain.
ISBN 0 517 69508 1
h g f d c b a

These pages: Lake Tahoe, California.

AMERICA
A VIEW FROM ABOVE

R. O. MATTHEWS

PORTLAND HOUSE

CONTENTS

INTRODUCTION

A great, sparkling ocean spreads out to the horizon, as it has done for millions of years. Sunlight catches the tips of the waves, reflecting in the same way that dazzled the earliest European settlers four centuries ago. But a thin ribbon of white spray on this vast sea betrays the presence of man. At the head of the ribbon, always pushing it forward as it disintegrates behind, is one of the many pleasure craft that sail the waters off the east coast of America.

On a warm summer morning the density of the craft surging out of the various harbors and inlets along the coast is astounding. They stream from the marinas around New York City like the spreading struts of some enormous fan, and return in the evening like a thousand white streamers sucked down a funnel. The multitude of craft which forms this feature of the summer scene on the Atlantic coast is an indication of the number of people who live in the land beyond. It is along this thin strip that perhaps the greatest concentration of humanity on the continent is found. Mighty cities crowd in upon one another, their suburbs almost touching. New York, Baltimore, Philadelphia, and a host of others, provide home and work for millions. At their centers the cities soar like man-made mountain crags to heights which make them a serious threat to any unwary bird – or aeroplane. Giant buildings rise sheer from the water's edge and dwarf the automobiles and buses that weave along the roads between them.

Out from the city hubs the dwellings become the low-lying structures associated with the commuter belt. Here the streets are broader and the buildings far from obvious from the air, partially hidden as they are beneath the branches of the trees which line and interweave the streets and roads. The suburbs would almost give the impression of endless tracts of untouched forest were it not for the freeways, which carve swathes through the land, and their junctions, which reveal centers of population.

The great interstate highways which run between major cities also twist inland across a landscape increasingly broken and rugged. The ground rises, first in low fluctuations, then in great ridges of rock, to form the mighty Appalachians. Running from the Atlantic and the Canadian border southwestward into the continent, the long, parallel valleys and peaks form one of the most distinctive landscapes in the east. The snow-capped summits of the highest mountains stand out like pristine napkins on the green and brown patchwork of the land.

Much used by skiing enthusiasts in the winter months, the mountains have been shaped to cater to the sport. Huge pathways down the slopes have been cleared of trees to provide an uninterrupted course where great speeds can be attained. During the summer months, however, when the crowds have gone with the snows, the fabulous ski runs are nothing more than scars on the dark forests which blanket the mountain slopes.

And beneath the dark forest canopy, flowing water catches the sunlight, reflecting it like myriad, ever-shifting mirrors. Leaping in sparkling cascades down the steep slopes, the babbling streams carry water from the melting snows and falling rain of the heights away on its long journey to the sea. Following age-old courses, far more ancient even than the mighty mountains, the streams run off in different directions. Long before the massive forces thrust the rocks upwards to form the Appalachian Mountains, rivers ran across the landscape of eastern America. As the beds of rock, thousands of feet thick, began to rise, twist and buckle, the rivers continued to flow. In some areas the torrent of water was so great that the rivers cut canyons and gullies along which to flow on their old courses as the mountains rose.

The brooks which fall down the western slopes of the Appalachians join to form broad, powerful rivers which snake away into the heart of the country. Growing in strength and power with every mile, the broad flows move ever southwestwards, collecting water from the land they pass and the countless streams which join them on their way. Winding between the farms, villages and towns of the valleys, for many years the rivers were the main transportation routes in these regions. When the first farmers crossed the Appalachians to escape the crowding of their fellows to the east, they moved their goods on flat-bottomed craft along the rivers, and in the north an artificial river, the Erie Canal, had later to be built to link them with the east coast.

As the white man moved on, lands to the south and west emerged from the wilderness and became more than blank spaces on the maps of the nation. The great rivers were traversed and mapped, and were found to be as good downstream as up. The broad ribbons of blue, which are today empty of all but the occasional pleasure craft, would then have been thick with smoke-belching monsters churning the river behind them. When the waters from the mountains join the flow which began far to the north at Lake Itasca, they create the most majestic river in the

The confluence of the Green and Colorado rivers in Canyonlands National Park, east Utah, where strange rock formations and Indian petroglyphs may be found.

nation, the wide Mississippi. Appearing as a great python enfolding fields and houses within its loops, it is still filled with commercial vessels on its lower courses and still snakes its tortuous path to the ocean as it always did. In New Orleans, the Mississippi throngs with barges and tugs, a feature of the river for miles downstream and upstream of the town.

Beyond the great north-south run of the Mississippi, other rivers reach out across land far different from that to the east. In place of the ridges and hills, revealing fresh views as each is passed, there is only the long, empty stretch of the plains. An unvarying panorama of flatness reaches westwards from the banks of the "Father of Waters." The rivers flow here, though, providing landmarks in an otherwise monotonous sea of waving grain and endless roads. Reflecting the square-mile system of land distribution in the last century, the roads meet at right angles and often take the long way round to a destination, rather than break their rigid, geometric pattern. Occupying these great squares and rectangles, bounded by roads and endless miles of barbed wire, are the spreading fields which comprise the Great Plains. During the long winter months the land lies barren beneath a blanket of snow, and the strict pattern of roads disappears beneath this frozen water. Even when the cold cloak of winter thaws, the land is brown and bare until the fresh, green shoots

poke between the clods. At first appearing as a green haze on the face of the plains, but then the grain grows until it covers the land almost as completely as the snow. When the green turns to gold and the gentle wind of late summer stirs the stalks, the plains almost disappear. The ground seems to twist and writhe as the air strokes the grain, turning it to an endlessly shifting haze on which it is almost impossible to focus.

But the Plains are not a huge single blanket of shifting grain. Scattered like islands are the marks of man: gas stations at intervals on the highways, and farm buildings, with their inevitable grain elevators, served by the ribbons of steel carrying the trains which make it all possible. As the Plains reach further and further to the south and west, features other than the roads and elevators mark the way. Huge rock formations rise sheer from the land. Many hundreds of feet high, Ship Rock stands alone on the broad expanse of the Plains. So tall and isolated are its features that guides leading wagons trains could navigate by them, in much the same way as sailors use stars. For days the rock would lie ahead of the wagons until they reached it, only to mark the horizon behind them for days more.

Eventually the monotony of the Plains breaks in the southwest in the face of geological forces so great they can hardly be imagined. Over a period of millions of years a great dome of rock, once covering parts of three states, was gradually lifted more than a mile into the sky, until the ancient, pre-Cambrian core of the continent lay far above sea level. Here, as in the Appalachians far to the

Gentle undulations in the pastureland of Palouse farming country, Washington, shelter the small, neat farmsteads that are characteristic of this region.

northeast, the old rivers in existence before the uplift were strong enough to continue on their old courses by cutting through the uplifting rock. But here there is a difference; there is only a small amount of rainfall and the climate is so severe as to allow little plant life. The low rainfall means that there is little erosion at work, other than the rivers, though the lack of vegetation creates a desert landscape in which wind-blown sand and grit can play a part in erosion far different from that played by water. Nevertheless, while the rivers have cut down, the upper levels have been left largely intact, and the sides of the valleys have not been rounded off by falling rain. The result is a vast network of canyons which criss-crosses the entire southwest. A seemingly level plain will suddenly drop away into an abyss so deep it staggers the imagination. More than a mile below sheer rock walls, a powerful torrent of silt-laden water will sparkle in the hot desert sun as it gouges out yet more rock.

The greatest of them all, of course, is the Grand Canyon of northern Arizona. The surging waters of the Colorado River have cut down through more than a mile of rock here, exposing the geological history of the area over more than a hundred million years. Elsewhere along its course the Colorado has been dammed by man to create vast reservoirs, but impressive as are the feats of man, they are nothing to the works of nature.

In other parts of the Southwest the arid conditions have created some of the most beautiful natural rock formations anywhere. In places, salt deposits underlie the surface rock, and when this is eroded by the constant drip of underground water, the surface features collapse. In the Needles District of Utah this has created long, parallel ridges of stone cut by deep, straight valleys. The minimal rainfall and the constant shifting of temperatures, together with wind-borne grit, have carved the soft rocks of the ridges into tortuous formations, while in places rock has been undermined and pierced to form natural bridges and arches.

Even the force which uplifted the dome of rock through which the canyons run is feeble compared to the earth convulsions which rocked the western states over a period of millions of years. When dinosaurs walked the earth, western North America was fairly low and level. Then the earth moved. Powerful earthquakes and volcanic eruptions, which still shake the region today, began to reshape the land. Fault lines opened up in the earth and massive sections of rock were moved. The geological history of the western states is complicated and violent, so much so that few scientists even pretend to understand what happened here. The results, however, are obvious.

Rising from the broad, flat expanse of the plains, a wall of rock climbs thousands of feet into the sky. Perhaps this effect is at its most dramatic in Wyoming, where the Teton Mountains leap from the valley of the Snake River like the walls of fairytale castles, complete with turrets and towers. Beyond the first dramatic wall of rock lie even taller, more rugged peaks to beckon the traveler. Romantic valleys lie hidden in the heart of the vast mountain ranges which unfold across the length of the continent. At Yosemite, incredibly tall and sheer mountains dominate a valley floor, a blanket of vegetation spread at their feet, while a thin trail of falling water marks the stream that is Yosemite's centerpiece.

The mighty Rockies are one of the most outstanding features of the land. They spread across more of the country, climb higher into the sky and plunge deeper into the earth than any other natural feature. In their highest reaches the mountains push so far into the thin atmosphere that the snow on their peaks never melts, and glaciers flow, inch by inch, down their flanks. In the mountain valleys, spread like green trails between the bare, rocky heights, flourish forests and meadows with a wildlife unique to the region: forests so impenetrable that they are rumored to be home to a creature often seen, but never captured – Bigfoot. Indeed, it is often these man-apes which are said to do the capturing, and more than one lone prospector has told how he has had to run for his life.

The same geological rendings which threw up the mountains had quite the opposite effect in a localized southern region of the Rockies. Here the pressures ripped away the support for a massive block of rock, which then simply sank into the depths of the earth. Surrounded by mountains many thousands of feet tall, Death Valley lies

The magnificent Hoover Dam, which lies on the border between Arizona and Nevada, is over 700 feet high and holds back the waters of Lake Mead, one of the largest artificial lakes in the world.

decidedly below sea level. Robbed of any rainfall by the peaks, the valley appears as a vast, flat, brown plain, almost devoid of life.

The mountains march on westward in endless ranks of majestic summits until they reach the sea. Here there is no broad plain, as in the east. The mountains just drop into the ocean and the land is at an end. The people who live here have to cluster around the few valleys which reach the ocean and cling to those hillsides not too steep to build upon. Constructed around its broad, natural bay, San Francisco enjoys perhaps the best site of them all. Yet even here the streets climb gradients unheard of elsewhere and the mountain wilderness is never far inland. To the west, the deep, swelling ocean runs unhindered and unbroken across hundreds of miles of empty scenery until the latest state in the Union comes into sight: Hawaii. Nestled in the bosom of the waters, these islands have the air of a paradise into which man has just wandered. From coast to coast and beyond, America is a beautiful country – a country which lies waiting to enchant each and every visitor.

MAINE

Sunshine over North Monmouth in the fall. This village, lying a little to the west of Augusta, the state capital of Maine, is typical of Kennebec County in its wooden houses of pastel shades, its simply constructed church and its setting amid trees and lakes. The valley of the Kennebec River is famous for such quiet, unassuming sites, whose beauty prompted the establishment of the Kennebec Valley Art Association, a group based in Augusta which finds its inspiration in this region.

MAINE

Right: Cape Elizabeth Lighthouse, near Portland, also known as Portland Headlight, and one of the oldest lights in the country. When its beacon was lit in January 1791, it became the first operational lighthouse under the new United States government. Today it is among just four authorized by President Washington that have never had to be rebuilt.

Above: one of the longest beaches on the Atlantic seaboard, at Old Orchard Beach, near Biddeford. Facing page: (top) coastline between Rockland and Spirit Island that exemplifies Maine, and (bottom) white houses, white boats in South Bristol Harbor.

MAINE

Left: Yarmouth, whose first English settlers, Anthony Thacher, John Crowe and Thomas Howes, arrived in April 1639. Thachers still own land in Yarmouth, some of which has been given to the town to be preserved as virgin woodland for ever. Top: the State House in Augusta, whose dome of 185 feet in height is distinctly "high-rise" in this town of long and low, rather than narrow and tall, buildings. Above: the tiny port of Friendship, famous for its Friendship sloop, a small fishing craft whose prowess is proven in the annual Friendship Sloop Races in July.

Their steep roofs an indication of the severity of the snowfall here each winter, the houses of Conway cluster on the banks of the Saco River, beside White Mountain National Forest. A major resort all year round, Conway caters for skiers in the winter and campers and hikers in the summer. Roads to the town from the north and west are some of the loveliest in the country.

Set amid immaculate lawns, the renowned Mount Washington Hotel at Bretton Woods is well placed and well equipped to cater for visitors to White Mountains National Park. One of few surviving hostelries from the last century, it was the site of the 1944 Bretton Woods Conference.

Above: the Mount Washington Cog Railway, whose tiny steam locomotive is almost as famous as the mountain itself. At over 6,000 feet, Mt. Washington is the highest peak in New England, and the railway is one of the best ways to reach its summit. The journey takes a leisurely hour and a half and, once there, there is always a chance that the usual fogs will clear and the summit's great fifty-mile vista of the White Mountains (left) will be apparent. Even without this bonus, the trip back down severe gradients is a memorable experience.

NEW HAMPSHIRE

Top: homesteads in Crawford Notch, a broad valley south of Mount Washington, in the heart of the White Mountains. North Conway (above) boasts a Russian-inspired railway station, the start of an eleven-mile-long scenic railroad through *the Saco River valley. Right: Concord, the state capital, whose buildings are complemented by the browns and greens of late fall foliage in this important commercial center on the banks of the Merrimack River.*

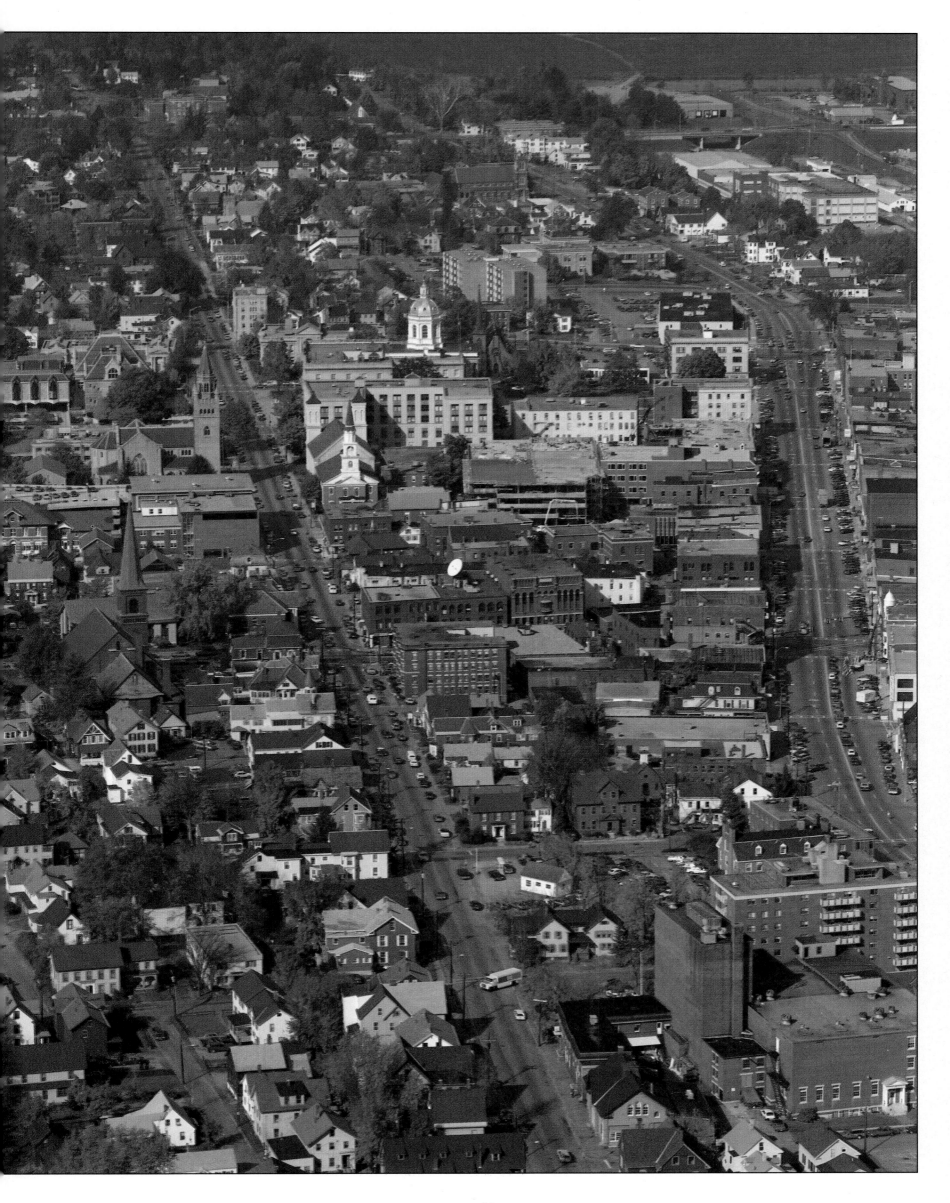

VERMONT

A river winds its tortuous course by a small town near Lake Champlain, a lake over 125 miles in length and the largest in the country after the Great Lakes. This stretch of water's beautiful surroundings have made it one of Vermont's most popular tourist destinations.

Above: Montpelier, the capital of Vermont, which lies on a hillside above the Winooski River. The State House (left) is constructed from granite, an appropriate choice since the granite industry was initially responsible for much of Montpelier's prosperity and growth; even today Vermont boasts the largest such industry in the nation. Farming is also of major importance to Vermont, and the sparkling dome, resplendent in fourteen-carat gold leaf, is crowned by a statue of Ceres, the goddess of agriculture.

VERMONT

It would be hard to exaggerate the beauty of the fall foliage in Vermont – indeed, people come from all over the country to experience these magnificent colors, which peak between early September and late October. The state takes these visitors very seriously, even providing a twenty-four-hour hotline to keep travelers informed of the progression of color in the forests.

VERMONT

Such a deep blue that they are almost black, a lake (facing page top) in the Walden Heights area and (left) another near to West Danville await the first frosts of winter. Once the town's trees are denuded of their leaves after the fall, the neat grid plan of the streets of Rutland (facing page bottom) can be clearly perceived from the air. Rutland, Vermont's second largest city, is famed for its marble; indeed, the stone for buildings as prestigious as the U.S. Supreme Court Building was quarried in this area.

Above: the forest clears to reveal houses near St. Johnsbury, where a swimming pool seems remarkably bright among the shades of green and gold. Vermont is sensitive to the importance of such unspoilt landscapes; billboards and neon signs have been banned by law.

VERMONT

Mud from the road turns snow the color of fudge in Killington, one of the state's major ski resorts, which boasts the longest ski lift in the world. For many, New England is now synonymous with skiing; certainly the facilities offered in Vermont for both downhill and cross-country skiing rank with the best in the world.

MASSACHUSETTS

The white spire of Old North Church,
Boston. It was here that Paul Revere had
lanterns lit to warn of the arrival of the
British Army. Old North Church has had
a special place in American hearts ever
since. The original spire was damaged in
a storm; this one dates from 1954.

Above: the slim, seemingly transparent John Hancock Building, which rises above the Back Bay area of Boston, one of the city's major shopping and residential areas. Left: the First Church of Christ, Scientist and the Christian Science Center. The religion of Christian Science was founded by Mary Baker Eddy, a New Hampshire woman who believed her serious malady had been healed as a result of her reading the New Testament. The movement's mother church stands in Boston, and Mary Baker Eddy's teachings are followed the world over.

MASSACHUSETTS

The perfect, sweeping curve of Cape Cod ends in the small settlement of Provincetown (left), once a whaling station. Today this area of fragile sand dunes, marshes and cliffs is protected by a division of the National Park Service, the Cape Cod National Seashore. Named for the great shoals of cod found there when it was discovered in 1602, the Cape was later visited by the Mayflower pilgrims prior to their landing at Plymouth in 1620. Top: Cape Cod's Nauset Beach and Pleasant Bay, and (above) Lighthouse Beach, with Eel Pond beyond, on Martha's Vineyard, an island lying across Nantucket Sound. Its strange name was given to it by the explorer Gosnold in 1602 in honor of his daughter. The abundance of wild vines then growing on the island had suggested a vineyard to him.

In an area of extremely flat terrain, Provincetown's 352-foot-tall Pilgrim Monument (above) can be seen for miles around. The Pilgrim Fathers arrived here by accident in winter, having been blown off course during a storm. They stayed for five weeks, exploring their seemingly barren, sandy surroundings, and then set sail again for the few days' voyage to Plymouth. Right: boats moored in Edgartown harbor, Martha's Vineyard.

Typical Cape Cod coastline near Brewster. Although the Cape provides the usual quota of motels, fast food outlets and souvenir shops, there remain stretches of coastline, acres of scrub oak forest and many sparkling lakes and ponds where visitors can "get away from it all."

RHODE ISLAND

Left: the incredibly convoluted shoreline around Brenton Point, Rhode Island, which is preserved as Brenton Point State Park. Here it is much quicker to use a row boat, rather than a car, to visit one's neighbor. In Newport (top), however, one's neighbor might have been a Vanderbilt or an Astor in this the summer resort of the very rich – so one might hesitate to call in such a humble craft! Around the turn of the century, millionaires started to build their versions of summer "cottages" in Newport. Inspired by the great palaces of Europe, these ostentatious residences dripped money and self importance. Above: Rhode Island State House, Providence, which is crowned with a dome fifty feet in diameter.

Above: high masts of fine yachts in Newport Harbor. The ultra-wealthy of this town were responsible for the development of yacht racing in the area before the First World War, and this ultimately led to the establishment of that great transatlantic yacht race, the America's Cup. Newport (right) has since been economically indebted to the Navy, whose presence is strong in the town.

Providence, the state capital, was founded
by Roger Williams, a dissenter who left
the Massachusetts Bay Colony as the
Puritans resented his criticisms of their
church. In return, he declared that his
colony would be a refuge for people
seeking freedom of worship, and so it was.

RHODE ISLAND

Elegant Newport Bridge, built in 1969, crosses Narragansett Bay to link Newport and Jamestown. Named for what was once the region's largest Indian tribe, the bay is the state's dominant natural feature, extending nearly thirty miles inland to divide Rhode Island nearly in half. Fine beaches, quiet coves and safe harbors abound along the 400 miles of state coastline – all the domain of yachtsmen, as Newport remains the sailing capital of the Atlantic seaboard.

CONNECTICUT

Left: City Hall, Hartford. Connecticut's capital city is unofficially recognized as the "Insurance Capital of the Nation," the industry having originated here in the eighteenth century when a group of men agreed to cover a shipowner's losses if his vessel sank. Since then, Hartford (below) has become home to more than forty insurance companies, which are responsible for many of the city's high-rises.

Distinctive beside the city's office blocks and skyscrapers (facing page bottom), Hartford's State Capitol (facing page top) stands resplendent, an unusual combination of Gothic Revivalism topped by a gold-encased, Classical dome. It was built in 1879.

Two fully rigged, original sailing vessels are the main attractions in the Mystic Seaport Museum at the mouth of the Mystic River. Here only the cars give away the fact that this is a reconstructed nineteenth-century port, rather than some forgotten backwater that chose not to modernize. The museum is the best-known feature of Mystic, a village which has been building ships since the seventeenth century.

CONNECTICUT

Above: leafless trees and gray-roofed houses crowd to the shore at Ocean Beach, not far from Harkness Memorial State Park (right), near New London. The house and grounds that constitute the park once belonged to the renowned philanthropist Edward Harkness, who inherited a fortune from his father and gave much of it away anonymously to hospitals, colleges and museums.

Mystic on a sparkling day in winter. In a boat-building center of some two hundred years standing, the people of Mystic have, over the years, constructed craft as diverse as whaling ships, clippers, pleasure boats, and vessels for the Navy during the Second World War.

Left: the city of Buffalo, an important port on Lake Erie. Home to large Canadian and Polish contingents, Buffalo is a cosmopolitan town that boasts some fine modern architecture. Below: deep greens highlight the red roofs of Mohonk Mountain House at New Platz, one of the finest hotels in southern New York State.

Niagara Falls (facing page top), the most famous waterfall in the world and probably the most spectacular, can be viewed at unnervingly close range from a sightseeing boat, the Maid of the Mist III (facing page bottom).

Like rivulets of molten lava, the streets of New York City glow throughout the night. From the very beginning, this great metropolis, which grew up around the finest harbor on the eastern seaboard, *comprised a diverse mixture of races and was unashamedly commercial in orientation. It remains so today, and as such is one of the nation's liveliest and most entertaining cities.*

NEW YORK STATE

Left: the twin towers of the World Trade Center, the world's second tallest structure after Chicago's Sears Tower, soar above Manhattan Island. Real estate in midtown Manhattan (above) is the most expensive in the world. Top: the 840 landscaped acres of Central Park bring the relief of green trees and blue water to the Island, where the Empire State Building – albeit no longer the tallest building in the world – still holds pride of place in the hearts of the city dwellers.

Above: Eaton's Neck, Long Island, where it really isn't far to walk to the beach! A thin strip of land known as Fire Island National Seashore lies off the southern side of Long Island and is connected to the main island by the Robert Moses Causeway, which spans Great South Bay. At the western tip of Fire Island lies Robert Moses State Park (right), named after the man who was responsible for establishing fourteen state parks on Long Island.

A solitary jetty stands in a serene setting in the Smithtown Bay area on the north coast of Long Island.

Fall colors near Trenton airfield. Trenton, the capital of New Jersey, was the scene of one of the most decisive battles of the American War of Independence. Eight miles from Trenton, Washington and the Revolutionary Army crossed the Delaware River in the middle of Christmas night, 1776. Although they were seen and a note of warning passed to Colonel Rall, the commander of the British troops in Trenton, so engrossed was Rall in the festivities that he pocketed the letter unread. When Washington arrived in Trenton the following morning, he found the British still sleeping. Victory was his.

NEW JERSEY

Trenton became the capital of New Jersey in 1790, and two years later its gold-domed State House was built. The city narrowly missed being the national capital: Congress was seriously considering Trenton after the town had been the temporary capital in 1784, but pressure from Washington and others in favor of a site on the Potomac changed their minds.

"Trenton Makes, the World Takes"
(above) was once a valid boast. Although
today the city's iron and rubber firms are
virtually all gone, Trenton still retains
the earliest of its industries, pottery.
Walter Lenox developed his famous china
in Trenton, causing the city to be known
as the "Staffordshire of America." The
potters remain in evidence and Lenox
china is still used in the White House
today. Left: a multi-arched bridge over the
powerful Delaware River.

Jersey City (facing page bottom and left) looks across the Hudson River to her big sister, New York City. It is possible to take a ferry from the city to Ellis Island and the Statue of Liberty. Strategically placed, Jersey City is a rail and sea terminus and a substantial industrial center. In contrast, Atlantic City (facing page top) is a comprehensive entertainment center, devoted to casinos, slot machines and night clubs.

Blessed by mild winters, Atlantic City (above) lies on a thin strip of land known as Absecon Island, whose potential as a resort site was first recognized in 1820, and realized when the Camden and Atlantic Railroad made Atlantic City its eastern terminus later in the century.

PENNSYLVANIA

The Golden Triangle of Pittsburgh, where the Ohio River is born out of the confluence of the Allegheny and the Monongahela. Not only the river, but Pittsburgh itself was born from this confluence, as this was the start of the route which commanded territory all the way to New Orleans. Various military forts were established here, the most recent being named after the British Prime Minister, Pitt – hence Pittsburgh.

PENNSYLVANIA

*Gettysburg National Military Park,
where fighting raged for three days until
the forces of the South under General Lee
were obliged to retreat. Part of the
Confederate defense of Philadelphia, it
was the bloodiest battle ever fought on
American soil: the combined casualties
exceeded 50,000.*

The thickly forested Pennsylvania Grand Canyon carved by Pine Creek. Situated in Tioga County, this fifty-mile-long gorge boasts walls that reach a thousand feet in some places. To the east lies Leonard Harrison State Park, while to the west can be found Colton State Park. Both these parks – areas where there are often more bears than people – provide the visitor with splendid vantage points from which to view the canyon.

PENNSYLVANIA

Left: the statue of William Penn, complete with Quaker hat, looks down upon his city from the heights of Philadelphia's City Hall. Penn faces northeast, towards Kensington, where he signed his treaty with the Indians upon arriving in Pennsylvania in 1682. Among a substantial number of Europeans who were to negotiate terms with Indians in the course of settling America, Penn was one of the few to keep his word. Top: the Gazelo Primeiro, moored at Penn's Landing, and (above) the Benjamin Franklin Parkway, named after the city's second most famous son.

DELAWARE

Highway 13 passing through Smyrna, a town in northern Delaware which takes its name from the Smyrna River. The Smyrna reaches Delaware Bay as the boundary of the Woodland Beach and Wildlife Area.

Left: the pleasingly neat grounds known as the Green that surround Delaware's State House in Dover. This white-roofed structure served as the state's capitol building until 1933. It has since been restored to its original 1792 appearance, and contains a large courtroom on the first floor, refurbished in every detail right down to the spittoons and spectacles. Above: typically flat farming country around Dover.

MARYLAND

This page: Baltimore, a city whose recent renaissance has made it one of the most delightful on the Eastern seaboard. For twenty years in the nineteenth century Baltimore deserved its reputation as "corrupt and content," as it was dominated by criminal political gangs which controlled the police and the legislature. By 1860, though, a reform movement had ousted those who had rigged elections and fueled riots, and Baltimore was on the mend. The extensive revitalization of the city during the past two decades, which has included a well designed redevelopment of its downtown area and the refurbishment of its older residential districts, is one of America's greatest urban success stories.

The Inner Harbor, Baltimore, where the
Constellation, *a ship built in 1797 that
operated until World War II, is moored.
Here too stands an electric entertainment
center, formerly a power plant, and the
National Aquarium, where sharks are
among the many exciting exhibits.*

MARYLAND

Annapolis, the capital city of Maryland, is dominated by the United States Naval Academy. Expanding to keep pace with the demands of the Fleet, the Academy has grown from its original ten acres of 1845 to 329 acres today. Throughout this time, its aim has been the same: "To prepare midshipmen morally, mentally and physically to be professional officers in the naval service."

MARYLAND

Below: the dignified blue and white buildings of the U.S. Naval Academy in Annapolis. Besides the Academy, Annapolis can boast over 300 eighteenth-century buildings, most of which have been beautifully preserved and serve to make this capital one of the most charming in the country. Bottom: Chesapeake Bay Bridge, which, though it *spans the Bay at its narrowest point, is still obliged to stretch for four miles. The traffic across it was so great that a parallel bridge was added in 1972. Right: white puffs of steam brighten the huge Bethlehem Steelworks at Sparrow Point, Baltimore, one of the most modern automated works of its kind.*

Above: Alexandria, one of the preferred suburbs of Washington, D.C. and a treasure trove of Georgian and early Federal architecture which has been faithfully preserved and lovingly maintained. Another Washington neighborhood (right), in the northwest part of the town, is not only a comfortable, charming place to live, but has the added advantage of being near Rock Creek Park, a 1,754-acre paradise where the wildflowers and wildlife could make a returning Algonquin Indian feel as though he were still in the seventeenth century.

The Washington Monument in Washington, D.C., a city of magnificent vistas. This marble structure is the tallest of its kind in the world. Completed in 1884, it was initially intended that the base be circled by a colonnade, but neither the funds nor the inclination for this materialized.

WEST VIRGINIA

As many trees as houses in a town in
northern West Virginia. This state is
considered to have some of the finest
mountain scenery east of the Rockies,
under which lies what are possibly the
richest coal seams in the world. West

Virginia is also rich in folklore and
musical and handicraft traditions, and the
art and craft fairs that are held all over the
state throughout the year attract much
attention.

VIRGINIA

Above: a red road snakes down to a farm near Greenfield in Nelson County. Greenfield lies on the edge of George Washington National Forest, which covers over a million acres and contains the highest waterfalls in the Blue Ridge Mountains. Right: the Magazine and Guardhouse in Williamsburg, southeast of the capital, Richmond. Williamsburg was itself the Colonial capital in 1699; today it is a living museum of restored and reconstructed eighteenth-century buildings.

In contrast to the mountainous regions in the west of the state, Virginian landscapes in the Chesapeake Bay area are flat, fertile and largely devoted to agriculture.

Facing page: the gently curving wake of a hidden boat contrasts with the rigid steel lines of the George Rogers Clark and J.F. Kennedy Memorial bridges in Louisville (above). The city is well known as the venue for the great Kentucky Derby, in which the finest bloodstock contests one of the world's most prestigious flat races on Churchill Downs each May. Left: the State Capitol, Frankfort. Built of Indiana limestone and finished in marble, this beautiful building is notable for its French influences. The rotunda is a copy of that which stands over Napoleon's tomb in the Hotel des Invalides, Paris, while the State Reception Room is a replica of Marie Antoinette's drawing room at Versailles, France.

Granted at least one tree for their shade, Kentucky thoroughbreds are given room to run on a typical stud farm near Lexington, the commercial center of the bluegrass region. Bloodstock breeding is a multi-million dollar business here, so these animals get the very best of care — for example, no paddock contains a sharp corner, so lessening the likelihood of one horse cornering another or injuring itself.

Left: the famous twin spires of the grandstand on Churchill Downs, Louisville, which are the "trademark" of the Kentucky Derby, and (below) a racetrack outside Lexington. In a state dedicated to the thoroughbred, it is possible to see horse racing in Kentucky – be it harness racing or flat racing – all year round.

Facing page: Lexington stud farms, where the paddocks are mown to ensure that the famous bluegrass remains short and sweet, and where the white-painted barns contain some of the world's fastest horses.

TENNESSEE

Left and top: downtown Chattanooga in sun and shade. Chattanooga was of considerable strategic importance during the Civil War, and several battles took place for its control. Federal forces finally occupied the city in 1863, and from here General Sherman began his infamous march through Georgia, leaving a trail of devastation behind him. Today the city is a headquarters for the Tennessee Valley Authority power system, and the University of Tennessee is also based in Chattanooga. Memphis (above), in the extreme southwest of the state, was named for the ancient Egyptian city because of its location on the great Mississippi River, which was considered analogous to the Nile in importance. Predictably, cotton is central to the city's economy, although Memphis also possesses flourishing manufacturing industries.

NORTH CAROLINA

Like an encroaching white sea, a bank of mist fills the valleys of the Great Smoky Mountains, where the national park and the Nantahala and Pisgah national forests attract thousands of visitors annually. As the soil here is poor, making agriculture unfeasible, and the geography of the district imposes isolation upon its small mountain communities, tourism has become the region's foremost industry.

Above: a farm near Raleigh, the state capital. Tobacco remains the primary North Carolina crop, and much of the state's wealth is derived from it. In addition, this state's textile industry is the nation's largest. Right: the State Capitol in Raleigh. Raleigh is named for the English adventurer Sir Walter Raleigh, who attempted to establish a colony in the state in the 1580s. Andrew Johnson, the seventeenth president of the United States, was born in Raleigh in 1808 and his home is preserved as a historic shrine.

An important educational center, Raleigh is home to North Carolina State University and numerous colleges, including St. Mary's (above). It is also part of North Carolina's Research Triangle, a three-county area of cultural, scientific and educational activities. The 5,500 forested acres of the Triangle encompass thirty agencies and firms, as well as the acclaimed Duke University Medical Center.

SOUTH CAROLINA

Right: the football stadium of the University of South Carolina (below) in Columbia. This university was opened as a college in 1805 and was one of few buildings to escape the devastating fire that swept through the capital after General Sherman's entry in 1865.

Facing page top: surrounded by very plain, modern architecture, Columbia's State House appears ornate by comparison. The walls were shelled in 1865 and the building was not completed until in 1907. A silver dome (facing page bottom) crowns a hospital on the outskirts of the city.

SOUTH CAROLINA

Appearing from the air like an emerald lying on dark green velvet, the immaculate paddocks of Coughman Farms, an extensive horse farm surrounded by forest, lie fifteen miles east of Columbia. Few regions of the United States have as long a history as the Southeast for breeding high quality horseflesh, and South Carolina ranks alongside Kentucky as a leading state in this pursuit.

Charleston's beautiful St. Michael's Episcopal Church was modeled upon St. Martin's-in-the-Field in Trafalgar Square, London. As such, it bears a Palladian Doric portico and a storied steeple, which rises 186 feet above the street. The venerable clock in the tower dates from 1764.

Above: the Battery area of Charleston, which contains a park displaying cannon and other relics from American wars. Their presence is a reminder that some of the settlement's earliest fortifications stood in this area. Charleston was the first permanent colony in the Carolinas, and here at Fort Moultrie was won the first decisive Patriot victory of the American War of Independence. Left: Coughman Farms, a stud farm near Columbia which, in its considerable size and grandeur, is an indication of the money to be made from horse breeding in this state.

GEORGIA

Atlanta, the phoenix-like capital of Georgia, rose from the flames of the Civil War to become one of the busiest and most successful capitals in the South. This is certainly not a traditional, moonlight-and-magnolia Southern town. It is a modern, vibrant city, very proud of itself and its achievements.

Stone Mountain, the centerpiece of Stone Mountain Park, which attracts nearly four million visitors each year. This, the world's largest mass of exposed granite, bears an enormous carving of Robert E. Lee, "Stonewall" Jackson and Jefferson Davis riding high and proud, heroes to the end.

The Coca-Cola Company's corporate headquarters in Atlanta form part of the backdrop to the city's 58,000-seat stadium (above), home to the Braves baseball and Falcons football teams. The drink Coca-Cola was invented in 1886 by an Atlanta pharmacist, John S. Pemberton, and was destined to be a phenomenal success. Left: the State Capitol, its dome covered in gold from a north Georgian mine. Its design is reminiscent, like that of so many capitols in the South, of the United States Capitol in Washington, D.C.

FLORIDA

Miami Beach, a popular island which lies three miles from Miami City across Biscayne Bay. Here are concentrated one quarter of the hotels in Florida, standing shoulder to shoulder since, in all, the island comprises only seven square miles of land. The most prestigious of these hotels face the Atlantic and offer private beaches, though, as erosion is a problem, sometimes these beaches are being gradually washed away.

FLORIDA

Miami Beach (these pages) is not all condominiums and luxury hotels. The Bass Museum of Art lies just off Dade Boulevard, quite near to the Theater of the Performing Arts. This museum contains a fine collection of paintings, sculpture and tapestries, while the theater complex is the chief outpost of Broadway hits. World-class concerts and ballet productions are also staged here. In all, it is hard to credit that a mere hundred years ago Miami Beach was simply a sand bar surrounded by mangrove swamps.

ALABAMA

At the end of Montgomery's elegant Dexter Avenue stands Alabama's State Capitol, white and dignified. On this site, Jefferson Davis was sworn in as president of the Confederate provisional government in 1861, when the city became the capital of the Confederacy. This is a fact Montgomery has not forgotten; her population remains proud of the South's fight for independence, and the city is full of cherished monuments and historic sites relating to its importance during the Civil War. Montgomery is recognized today as a manufacturing center, and also claims the largest livestock market in the Southeast, which contributes to its position as the focal point of the state's agricultural trade.

MISSISSIPPI

Right: Jackson, Mississippi's state capital. After a fateful day in May 1863, when the Union's General Sherman gave orders that everything of value in the city should be burnt, Jackson was known for a time as *Chimneyville – little in the town was left standing. Today, however, the rebuilt Jackson is handsome and dignified, its State Capitol (above) a noble building of elegant proportions built in 1903.*

111

MISSOURI

Left: the splendid Busch Memorial Stadium in St. Louis, which is possibly the most football-conscious city in the country. The stadium, the home of the Cardinals baseball and football teams, was completed in 1966 and seats 50,000 people. Its ultra-modern design allows unobstructed viewing from any part – and possesses a particular beauty, too. Rolling hills, tree-lined boulevards and numerous parks combine to make Kansas City (below) one of the most attractive in Missouri.

Facing page top: six Ionic columns on the University of Missouri campus in Columbia, which includes the original campus of the university, the oldest state university west of the Mississippi, founded in 1839. Columns also feature in the State Capitol (facing page bottom) in Jefferson City – 134 of them in all.

MISSOURI

The enormous, simple, yet unforgettable arch known as the Jefferson National Expansion Arch in St. Louis. Encased in stainless steel, the structure is the tallest monument in America, surpassing, at 630 feet, even the Washington Monument. The Arch symbolizes St. Louis' position in history as the "Gateway to the West" and is built, appropriately, on the site of an eighteenth-century trading post.

The French Quarter, known as the Vieux
Carré, of New Orleans. The narrow
streets remain as they have been for many
years, the sound of jazz resounds about
wrought iron railings, while squares –
vieux carré is French for "old square" –
provide a cool respite from the bustle of
the city.

New Orleans, the first great city on the Mississippi-Missouri river system and the largest in Louisiana. Its busy harbor is the foundation of its primarily commercial economy, although the city's manufacturing industry is growing. New Orleans' restaurants are world famous for their Creole specialties, while the city as a whole is renowned for its annual winter celebration, the spectacular, joyous Mardi Gras.

LOUISIANA

New Orleans' Greater New Orleans
Bridge mirrored by a second, such is the
demand to cross the Mississippi River at
this point. When it was built in 1958, this
bridge had the longest cantilevered span
of any such bridge in the United States.

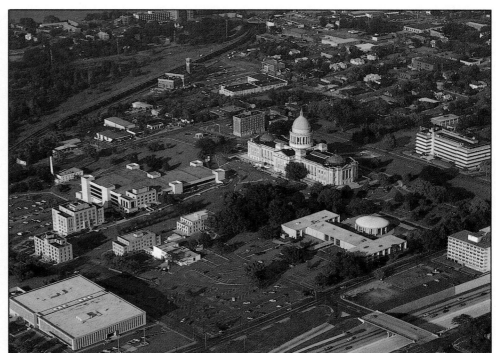

Left: slow and wide, the Arkansas River makes its stately progress towards the capital of Little Rock, which lies almost exactly at Arkansas' center. The river dissects the state diagonally as a major tributary of the Mississippi, which forms the state's eastern border. Little Rock (above) only became a river port in 1969, however, when a system of dams and

locks connected the city properly to the Arkansas River. Top: the city of Hot Springs, which lends its name to a national park that lies on its northwestern perimeter. Only an hour's drive from Little Rock, Hot Springs is a city of thermal baths and spas that, as a popular health resort, attracts thousands of visitors annually.

ILLINOIS

Lake Shore Drive, Chicago, where Lake Michigan stretches away like a sea. Although Chicago is a vast commercial center, its population has not forsaken art and science – instead it has combined them with commerce: Chicago boasts some of the nation's most innovative and exciting architecture.

This page: the Chicago skyline. This city is world famous as the home of the tallest building on earth, the Sears Tower, which rises to the incredible height of 1,468 feet and has a power requirement equal to that of the state's second largest city, Rockford. Alongside such stunning skyscrapers, Chicago can also boast a considerable collection of plaza art. Sculptures on permanent display include works by Picasso and Calder, while First National Plaza contains a seventy-foot-long mosaic by Chagall.

ILLINOIS

The Chicago River divides downtown Chicago. In the nineteenth century this river flowed into Lake Michigan, but it carried so much pollution from the city that it was resolved in 1885 that the river's course should be reversed.

Undaunted by the enormity of the task, Chicago engineers performed the largest earth-moving operation the country had ever seen, and today the river ultimately joins the Mississippi.

The Indianapolis Motor Speedway (left), built in 1909, is today one of the most famous tracks in the country, as it is here that the annual Indianapolis 500 Motor Race is held. The race regularly attracts crowds of up to 300,000 people and is run for a prize of $1,500,000. The state capital, Indianapolis is a prosperous city: situated at the heart of the Corn Belt, it boasts a leading grain market and is the hub of the region's road, rail and air transport. The elegant, gray and white State Capitol (above) now stands alongside some excitingly futuristic architecture, yet its design remains as commanding and as dignified as it was upon completion in 1888.

The gleaming octagons and cylinders of
Detroit's Renaissance Center, known as
the "Ren Cen." Rising above all is the
tallest hotel in the world, the circular
Detroit Plaza. At seventy-three stories,
this, the highest building in Michigan,
looks down on the rest of Detroit, too.

Above: Belle Island, most of which is devoted to a substantial park. The island boasts a zoo, an aquarium and a botanical garden, and in the summer offers outdoor symphony concerts. It has long been a favorite spot for Detroit family excursions. Left: downtown Detroit, where the distinctively russet-colored National Bank of Detroit stands apart from its concrete-gray brethren.

OHIO

Lake Erie glows like molten copper in the light of a sunset over Toledo, Ohio's major port on the Great Lakes. Toledo was settled permanently after the War of 1812, and twenty-three years later both Michigan and Ohio claimed the desirable small town, almost coming to blows over the matter until President Jackson settled the issue in favor of Ohio. Today the city is one of the largest in the state and is highly industrial.

WISCONSIN

Church spires and chimney stacks surround Madison's regal State Capitol. This imposing building and the city's business district stand on a narrow neck of land between two of southern Wisconsin's larger lakes, Mendota and Monona. Landscaped parks and lakesides and tree-lined avenues are characteristic of this city. Although manufacturing is starting to broaden Madison's economy, the University of Wisconsin and government departments based here are the major employers, their presence granting the capital an air of quiet sophistication.

WISCONSIN

Facing page top: the isthmus upon which Madison stands, a beautiful setting which the capital has done much to enhance, and (facing page bottom) the university football stadium. The University of Wisconsin owns a thousand-acre campus fronting Lake Mendota, a location considered to be one of the nation's loveliest for the purpose. Left: the heavily forested Dells Region in central Wisconsin, through which flows the great Wisconsin River. En route, this deep river has carved a variety of unusual shapes in its sandstone banks, and the Dells Region is famous for these imaginatively named forms, such as Black Hawk's Head and the Devil's Elbow.

Above: Wyalusing State Park, one of the prettiest in Wisconsin. Situated beside the Mississippi and Wisconsin rivers, Wyalusing is rich in wildlife, its varied geography providing habitats for deer, fox and raccoon in the uplands, while beaver and mink find shelter in the floodplain areas.

IOWA

Iowa as the locals love it – acres of the finest topsoil immaculate in their cultivated livery near Des Moines. Iowa, translated from the Indian, means "beautiful land," and certainly, so rich a prairie could be nothing less in the eyes of a farmer.

137

IOWA

Des Moines, both the largest city in the state and the state capital, is flat and full of greenery, like much of Iowa itself. Situated at the confluence of the Raccoon and Des Moines rivers, the city is the center of Iowa in many ways – it is set in the geographical center of the state, and is the Iowan industrial, agricultural, retail and financial center too. All roads lead to Des Moines, whose name is derived from its position midway between the Mississippi and Missouri rivers.

On a gentle hill in Des Moines, the gold dome of Iowa's State Capitol (above) stands ornate and shining against the matt, rectangular office blocks that form downtown Des Moines (left). The wealth of parkland and trees spread out before the Capitol is just a suggestion of some of the fifty-eight recreation areas in and around Des Moines. As one might expect, this city is surrounded by wheat, and not far to the west of the capital lie the Living History Farms. Three fully operational farms are featured here for the enlightenment of numerous visitors: a pioneer farm of the 1840s, a 1900 horse-powered farm and a farm of the future.

MINNESOTA

The high-rises of Minneapolis dominate the eastern shore of the Mississippi River. The name "Minneapolis" is derived from the Sioux Indian word for water, minne, and the Greek for city, polis, and the name is indeed apt. Water was important in the city's development, which initially centered upon the Falls of St. Anthony. At first these falls were harnessed to produce power for a flour mill serving nearby Fort Snelling, and later the Mississippi was used to transport logs, enabling the once-small village of St. Anthony to become a sizeable lumber town by the mid-nineteenth century. When St. Anthony amalgamated with nearby Minneapolis in 1872, a great city was born.

MINNESOTA

Right and facing page top: St. Paul, "last city of the East" and the state capital of Minnesota. St. Paul is conservative, traditional in outlook and generally a far quieter city than its twin across the Mississippi River. It is certainly culturally lively, however. Although St. Paul does not boast a theater as illustrious as Minneapolis' Guthrie Theater – one of the most famous in the country – , the St. Paul's Arts and Science Center is a fascinating modern complex, featuring sculpture, paintings and Egyptian mummies, while the city's Chimera Theater presents musicals, dramas, and special plays for children all year round.

A bustling, vibrant town, today Minneapolis (above and facing page bottom) is the hub of the wheat market and, like Des Moines, is the commercial and industrial center of a vast agricultural area – the city's grain exchange is the world's largest cash grain market.

MINNESOTA

Minneapolis, which has twice been voted the "All-American City," its record of enlightened industrial progress, its cultural achievements and its sensitive program of urban renewal having impressed many far beyond the borders of Minnesota. This city has reason to be proud of itself ecologically, too: within its limits lie twenty-two lakes, all healthy enough to support a wide variety of fish.

NORTH DAKOTA

Top: the State Capitol towering above the North Dakota capital of Bismarck (above), which was named for the German Chancellor in the hope that this would induce Germany to invest in transcontinental railroads – at the time the town was the terminus of the Northern Pacific Railway. In 1875 a gold rush centering upon the nearby Black Hills brought prosperity to Bismarck as the town supplied equipment to eager prospectors, and since then it has grown steadily. Right: the restored blockhouses of Fort Abraham Lincoln in the state park of the same name, near Bismarck. It was from here that General Custer left for Montana and his fatal confrontation with Sitting Bull. Much of the wealth of South Dakota is still derived from the land: the state is rich in wheat, oil, gas and lignite.

SOUTH DAKOTA

A strip of rich, black soil cuts a swathe through wheat stubble on a Walworth County farm. South Dakota experiences savage extremes of temperature: winter can send the thermometer plummeting to -40°F, while summer may inflict a searing 110°F. There are still those on the land whose grandparents would have seen sod houses on the prairie and gold rushes in the Black Hills – days when the state was just beginning.

SOUTH DAKOTA

Left: the characteristically dry, serrated peaks of Badlands National Park in the southwest of the state. This national park, created in 1978, comprises an area of stark, seemingly barren ridges, buttes and spires of sandstone. An almost unearthly landscape, the Badlands are devoid of vegetation but rich in fossils – the remains of three-toed horses and sabre-toothed tigers have been found here. Today they are home to coyotes, prairie dogs and jackrabbits.

Facing page top: the falls on the Big Sioux River, where settlers were harried by the Sioux, the tribe fiercest in resisting white incursion. Even the Sioux could not hold back the tide, however, and Sioux Falls (facing page bottom and above) grew to be South Dakota's largest city.

NEBRASKA

The Nebraska State Capitol in Lincoln. Completed in 1932 and looking faintly like a rocket on its launch pad, the central tower of this avant-garde building rises 400 feet and has long been recognized as one of the world's architectural masterpieces. The capital of Nebraska, Lincoln was originally called Lancaster, but was renamed in honor of President Lincoln when it became the state capital in 1867, the year of Nebraska's statehood. At that time the small town contained only thirty residents – today it has a population of nearly 200,000.

NEBRASKA

Omaha (above) was named for the tribe of Indians who made way for white settlers after signing a treaty in 1854. The young town was a fairly lawless place – gunfights in the streets were the norm and lynching a common, rough and ready form of "justice." By 1879, however, Omaha was sufficiently civilized to be the site of an historic trial that recognized the American Indian as a human being, with rights under the Constitution. Since those days, the town has grown into the largest city in Nebraska and can boast the biggest livestock market in the world – Nebraska is still cowboy country. Right: Rosenblatt Stadium, Omaha, where the NCAA College Baseball World Series is held annually.

Above: lush farmland between Lincoln and Omaha, typical of southeast Nebraska. Petroleum is the state's main mineral resource, while ninety-five percent of the land is devoted to agriculture and most Nebraskan manufacturing industries are connected with farming.

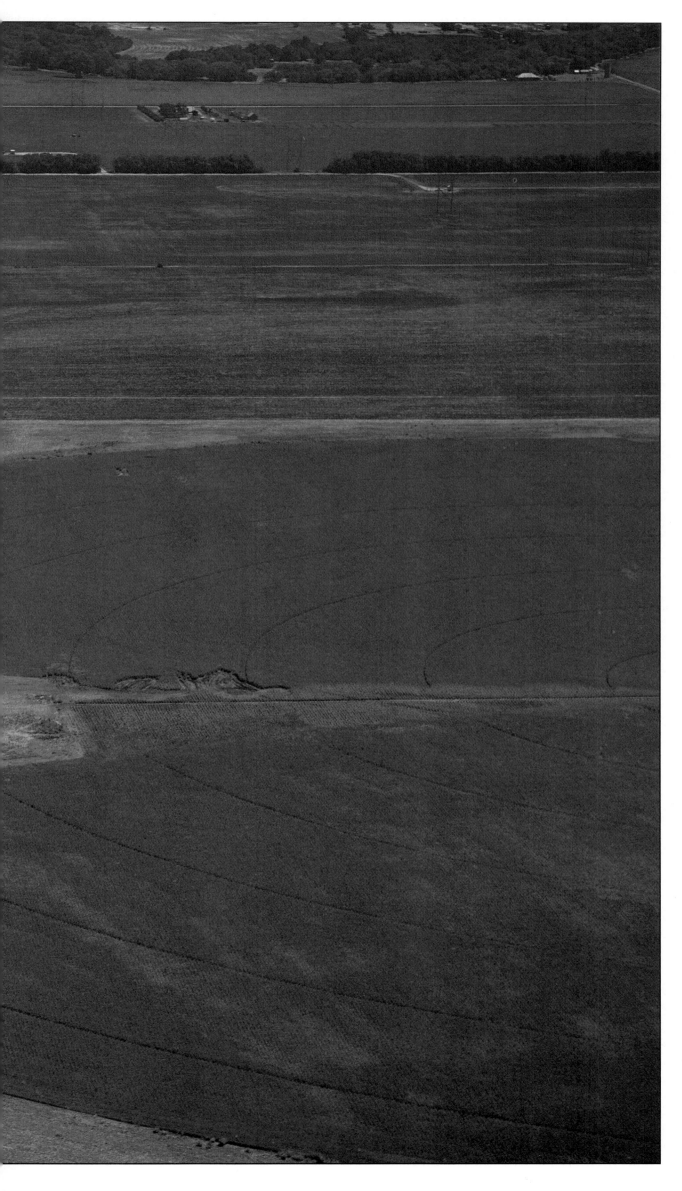

KANSAS

Left: farmland near Wichita, the state's largest city, in southern Kansas. Kansas is the United States' foremost wheat and sorghum producer and its third most important source of beef and veal. These statistics, impressive though they are, cannot, however, reveal the extent to which this state lives and breathes farming. Four hundred miles long by two hundred miles wide, Kansas comprises virtually continuous fertile prairie, and ninety percent of this is farmed. Only a hundred years ago, a man could ride for days across this land through grass as high as his stirrups. Today the cultivation of cereal crops takes precedence, and farms of 1,200 acres are the norm, many being substantially larger.

KANSAS

Though Wichita (above) contains some of the world's largest grain elevators, and more wheat is milled here than anywhere else in the state, the city is best known for the production of aircraft, its three plants building more light aircraft than all the other cities in the nation combined. Right: the circular results of pivotal irrigation are evident in the farmland of southern Kansas, where 130-acre fields of alfalfa or grain are watered from wells, a system which can provide up to ten harvests a year.

Kansas' "black gold" – some of the
world's most fertile soil. Despite this
asset, the farmer's life is a hard one, as the
weather can be harshly unpredictable.
Vital summer rain may not arrive, while
apple-sized hailstones may fall in August
– ruining a year's work in an hour.

OKLAHOMA

An immaculate Oklahoma farm, punctuated by white fences and red roofs, lying north of Oklahoma City. Oil is Oklahoma's fundamental source of wealth, but much of the land is under the plough and wheat is the state's leading cash crop.

Above: downtown Oklahoma City, the state capital, which was settled virtually overnight when the territory was opened to white homesteaders during the last century. Situated on the banks of the North Canadian River, Oklahoma City is one of the largest cities in land area in the country. At the height of the oil boom about 1,400 oil wells were producing oil within the city limits, and the petroleum industry remains of major economic importance. The city is also one of the nation's foremost aviation centers, a major transportation and distribution point, and can boast possibly the finest zoo in the Midwest. Left: the State Capitol complex, which actually has an oil well beneath it.

OKLAHOMA

Northern Oklahoma farms, whose rich browns and greens belie the troubled agricultural history of this part of the state. In the Twenties, drought and wind confirmed the errors of over-planting and over-grazing by eroding the soil on a massive scale. Harvests failed, cattle died and thousands of tenant farmers were obliged to move on or starve in the dustbowls that had been created. Today the farms are larger and the dangers of such devastating erosion are known and largely avoided, enabling Oklahoma to grow and rear some of the country's finest agricultural produce.

163

Above: jets cluster around one of many terminals like bees around a honey pot at the Dallas-Fort Worth Regional Airport, held to be among the five safest in the world. Opened in 1974, this, the largest commercial airport in the world, covers a Manhattan-size area, its dimensions reflecting the scale of the city's development in recent years. Another exciting feature of this "can do" city is the Wet and Wild Waterpark (right), which lies just off Interstate 30 near Dallas.

Dallas' Reunion Tower, reminiscent of a giant microphone, which houses a revolving restaurant and cocktail lounge. Situated between the Hyatt Regency Hotel and the Reunion Arena, the tower is the focal point of the Reunion area, a nineteenth-century French immigrant settlement.

TEXAS

Albeit more relaxed in its general attitude than its near neighbor, Fort Worth (above and right) is one of Texas' major centers for oil and livestock. It is also renowned for its fine collection of museums and galleries. As its name would suggest, the city was initially a military camp, named after one General Worth, a hero of the Mexican War. Like Dallas, it was founded beside the Trinity River but, before the coming of the railroad in 1876, it looked to be a sleepy backwater – indeed, it was dubbed "Pantherville," as it was said to be so quiet that a panther slept though the night in Main Street. Today, the closest a panther could get to bustling Main Street would be a bed in Fort Worth's Zoological Park. Top: one of two White Water parks between Dallas and Fort Worth whose features, such as a Spanish galleon and a wave pool, are immensely popular with children.

Corpus Christi has a diversified economy in which both natural gas and seafood play prominent roles. Blessed with a deep water port, the city is built around Corpus Christi Bay, which was discovered by a Spanish explorer, Alonzo de Pineda, on the feast of Corpus Christi in 1519.

TEXAS

The San Jacinto Monument, which marks the spot near Houston where Texas won her freedom from Mexico in 1836. The Texan victory was total – it took longer to count the dead and prisoners than to win the battle: this was over in twenty minutes, partly because the Texans attacked during the Mexican siesta.

Above: oil refineries lining the waterway in Corpus Christi. Texas contributes a third of the nation's total production of crude oil and natural gas. Left: downtown Houston, this vast state's largest city – indeed, the largest in the South. Named after Texas' most revered hero, and founded in the same year as the Texan Republic, 1836, Houston is rich and modern. Here the numbers of privately owned planes and yachts rival the number of household cars, while the location of the Lyndon B. Johnson Space Center just outside the city means Houston is ideally placed to exploit the new ideas and products generated by the space programs.

NEW MEXICO

ARIZONA

Right: the ruins at Fort Union National Monument, on the old Santa Fe Trail northeast of the state capital of Santa Fe. Fort Union protected part of the Santa Fe Trail for forty years, and many settlers and travelers along the trail owed their lives to its presence. The trail itself was an important trade route, operational throughout the last century between Missouri and New Mexico.

Below: Tucson, famous as a winter resort and Arizona's second most important city after Phoenix. Situated in the south of the state in a desert valley, thereby enjoying a dry and sunny climate, the city has a reputation as a healthy place to live. Bottom: streets stretch to the horizon in the industrial and cultural center of Phoenix, state capital of Arizona.

ARIZONA

Left: the inhospitable terrain of the Black Canyon below the Hoover Dam, in the northeast of the state. One of the largest dams in the world, the Hoover Dam – originally called Boulder Dam, but later named for the President in office at the time of its construction – created vast Lake Mead, one of the largest lakes in the country. Spanning the border between Arizona and Nevada, the lake is the centerpiece of a substantial recreation area. Top: tennis courts lining the Arizona Canal, a feature of the Biltmore Fashion Park in central Phoenix. Phoenix (above), lying just south of the state's center, was built on the banks of the Salt River in a semi-arid valley. Salt River irrigation projects were largely responsible for the town's growth during the late nineteenth century, though today agriculture is second to manufacturing industries in its importance to the city's economy.

175

ARIZONA

The distinctive finger of Spider Rock in Canyon de Chelly National Monument, northeast Arizona. Here smooth, red sandstone walls rise sheer for as much as a thousand feet from the canyon's twenty- *six-mile-long floor. Ruins of houses built in these cliff faces by the Pueblo Indians can still be seen; there are more than sixty such sites to explore in the canyon, some of which date from 306 AD.*

ARIZONA

These pages: the Grand Canyon. In 1857, American lieutenant Joseph Ives said of the canyon "It is altogether valueless ... Ours has been the first and will doubtless be the last party of whites to visit this profitless locality." Today this incredible scarring by the Colorado River across the high plateaux of northwestern Arizona is considered to be a sight every American should endeavor to experience – and certainly the Grand Canyon is one of the most breathtaking geological phenomena in the world. A mile deep and in some places eighteen miles wide, the canyon is over two hundred miles long. Each moment of the day the light shifts subtly to change the colors of the rock and lengthen or shorten the shadows, thereby revealing some new detail.

Above: Moab, which lies in the desert at the southernmost point of Arches National Park, at the foot of the La Sal Mountains. The town has been a thriving community since the discovery and mining of uranium in the area after the Second World War. Right: the State Capitol in Salt Lake City. Built in 1916 from Utah granite and Georgian marble, it commands an extensive view of the valley in which the city shelters.

Surrounded by greenery, the City and County Building stands in Romanesque splendor on Washington Square in Salt Lake City. For almost twenty years it served as the state's Capitol – an appropriate site, as it was in Washington Square that arriving Mormons made camp in 1847. Since then, the city they created beside the Wasatch Mountains has grown into one of the most beautiful in the land and one of the richest in the region. The state symbol of the honeybee was chosen to indicate the industry of the Mormons, and their diligent application has reached its apogee in the development of Salt Lake City.

UTAH

Punctuating with green the creams and golds, the spires of Douglas fir line up in gullies to be dwarfed by the thin, ridged columns that are the central feature of Bryce Canyon National Park in southern Utah. The park, one of the state's most spectacular, was established in 1928; through most of the previous century it had been considered merely as a "hell of a place to lose a cow." As in the Grand Canyon, which lies across Utah's southern border, the color of the rocks in Bryce Canyon seem to alter hourly, being particularly entrancing at dawn and late afternoon, when they seem almost iridescent.

COLORADO

Right: grid-plan streets bring a sense of geometric order amid a wilderness of snow and rock in the mountain town of Aspen, initially a silver-mining center but today a renowned ski resort, the largest in the country. Its popularity is due to its surrounding slopes (below), which promise some of the finest powder *snow found anywhere. Bottom: the resort of Vail, which many claim rivals St. Moritz in its facilities and design – here are slopes "built by skiers for skiers." Created as a Tyrolean Alpine village in a sheep meadow in 1962, today Vail is the most successful ski village in Colorado.*

COLORADO

The financial center of "mile high" Denver, the state capital that lies on the Great Plains a mile above sea level, beside the Rocky Mountains. A mining camp of a mere twenty-five cabins in 1858, the city grew during the last century as a result of rises in the price of gold and silver.

Above: a sandstone monolith and part of the ridge that comprise the 940-acre park known as the Garden of the Gods, in Colorado Springs (left), Colorado's most popular summer resort. Lying south of Denver, this, the state's second largest city, was named after Manitous Springs and Colorado City, its predecessor. A military center, this is the home of the U.S. Air Force Academy, Fort Carson and Peterson Air Force Base. To the south, the city can also boast the World Arena, which hosts many Olympic skating events.

COLORADO

Nestling at the edge of Pike National Forest, Colorado Springs was founded in 1871 by General Palmer, builder of the Denver and Rio Grande Western Railroad, as a summer playground and health resort. The town has blossomed into a beautiful cultural center and a year-round resort, but its initial development was slow; it took the discovery of gold at nearby Cripple Creek in the 1890s to bring Colorado Springs to public attention.

WYOMING

Top: the State Capitol in Cheyenne (above). Built of sandstone and crowned by a gold dome fifty feet in diameter, this neo-classical building can be seen for many miles. Cheyenne itself was named for the Indian tribe removed to make way for the arrival of the Union Pacific Railroad in 1867. In the last century the town, then a lawless place ruled by vigilantes, was primarily a center for cattle shipment and mining supplies, and even today Cheyenne depends upon the cattle and sheep market for part of its livelihood. Now, however, there is also trade in timber, oil and coal, and a blossoming tourist industry, which is hardly a surprise as Wyoming is a breathtakingly beautiful state. Right: the serene Snowy Mountains, part of Medicine Bow National Forest in Laramie County.

WYOMING

Facing page: a startlingly dark blue river meanders through a meadow in the Red Mountain region of Yellowstone National Park, where stands of timber are felled to make way for new growth (above). Nine national forests lie wholly or partially within the state, and lodgepole pine, spruce and some fir constitute the bulk of timber taken, under Forest Service guidance, from these areas. Left: strip farming west of Cheyenne, designed to conserve water and prevent soil erosion in this semi-arid region. Dry farming of this type, aided by ever-expanding irrigation projects, produces not only wheat, barley and corn, but also potatoes, alfalfa, sugar beet and beans.

WYOMING

A staggered network of conveyor belts transports shale, a rock formed from clay from which oil is extracted, across an oil shale pit near Cheyenne. Wyoming not only leads all other states in coal reserves, it also produces fifty percent of the Rocky Mountain region's crude oil – indeed, it is oil that forms the basis of the state's economy.

MONTANA

Macdonald Creek and the towering face of Garden Wall in Glacier National Park – aptly named, as there are some forty glaciers among the peaks in this region of northwestern Montana. Although it would appear deep in untouched wilderness, a highway known as Going-to-the-Sun Road runs parallel to Garden Wall, whose forbidding bulwark makes it one of the country's most impressive mountain routes.

197

IDAHO

IDAHO

Left: cleared runs between the trees on a hill north of Boise indicate the presence of a winter ski resort. Most Idaho ski areas are found within national forest boundaries and the state is rich in such forests – indeed Idaho's most famous resort, Sun Valley, lies between two of them, Challis and Sawtooth.

Facing page top: a crop patchwork in the valley of the Snake River, a fertile area in southwest Idaho. Facing page bottom and above: Boise, the capital and the financial heart of Idaho, which takes its name from the French for wood, bois, the name given to this site by French trappers.

IDAHO

A view of agricultural land southwest of Boise, ribboned by a solitary road and many irrigation ditches, has the appearance of an abstract painting. Large irrigation projects have turned dry lands into productive fields here, and although Idaho is largely comprised of great mountains, deserts and forests, it is for the impressive fertility of this corner that the state is best known.

IDAHO

These pages: fields of wheat and potatoes blanket the southwestern corner of the Gem State. Though it is known nationwide for the quality of its potato crop, neither this nor any other crop would have been possible without the presence of the Snake River, whose *plentiful waters are the source of irrigation upon which the state's agriculture depends. Three-quarters of Idaho's population is supported by this irrigated land, and therefore, indirectly, by the Snake and its tributaries.*

WASHINGTON

Left: the Palouse River passing through its bleak canyon of scree and sagebrush on its way to join the Snake River in the southeastern corner of the state. The Palouse, one of many rivers that have carved their courses deep into the region's basalt plateau, forms the main attraction of Palouse Falls State Park, where its waters drop a sheer 198 feet into a large, *dark pool. Above: farms in the Green River region. Before the Green River is transformed into the Durwamish and empties into Elliott Bay in central Seattle, it passes through superb farmland, some of which contributes towards Washington's position as the country's premier apple producer.*

WASHINGTON

Built upon hills between Lake Washington and Puget Sound, Seattle (above) is the metropolis of the Pacific Northwest, its fine, protected harbor, Elliot Bay, serving to make the city one of the world's great seaports. Laid out in 1853 by trappers and lumberjacks, the settlement had a slow start as there was a great shortage of women in this remote corner of the continent. In desperation, one intrepid gentleman went East and persuaded eleven eligible ladies to return with him to Seattle and thereby promptly reduced the ranks of bachelors by that number. His success led to the importation of a hundred Civil War widows – and modern Seattle was on its way. Right: luxury houses meeting Lake Washington in Bellevue, and (facing page) the Space Needle, the symbol of Seattle.

A lone boat crosses Elliot Bay, past the high-rises of downtown Seattle. The city was named for an Indian chief, who initially objected to the honor on the grounds that his eternal rest would be disturbed whenever his name was mentioned. The settlers finally agreed to the canny chief's request that they pay him a tax as advance compensation for his troubled sleep – so Seattle it was, at a price!

Much of the controversial Alaskan oil pipeline (facing page) was built above ground to avoid melting the permafrost of the tundra and so upsetting its delicate ecological balance. In use since 1977, the pipeline stretches from Prudhoe Bay down the length of the state to Valdez, and is widely considered to be vital to the Alaskan economy. The Chugach Range forms the icy, but beautiful, backdrop to Anchorage (above), the state's largest city, made larger by the discovery of oil. Left: Mount McKinley, at 20,320 feet the United States' highest peak, majestic in its marbling of snow.

ALASKA

Part of the vast Harding Icefield, which spawns over thirty glaciers from its position in the Kenai Mountains, near Seward, on the Kenai Peninsula. The field, which covers more than 850 square miles and is partly included in the Kenai Fjords National Park, is the result of the winter snowfall in these mountains exceeding the amount that melts in summer. As a layer of snow is buried by subsequent falls, it is gradually transformed into ice. When part of the field – in the form of a glacier – meets the sea, there is a thunderous cracking sound as the ice cliffs break and fall; Alaskans say that the glacier is calving.

The serene waters of Aialik Bay (top) wash the feet of the Kenai Mountains as they meet the sea near Seward. Reaching over 6,500 feet in height, these peaks surround the Harding Icefield, allowing only narrow channels for the glaciers the field engenders to slink down to the waves. Incised by Arctic winds, ice compacts to form the relentless frozen river that is Ruth Glacier (left), on the flank of Mount McKinley. Moving imperceptibly – on average three feet a day – and quite unstoppable, the glaciers of Mount McKinley National Park (above) are some of the most impressive in Alaska.

OREGON

The last snows of spring concede to summer on Wizard Island in Crater Lake, the centerpiece of Crater Lake National Park. The island, a cinder cone, is a reminder of the forces that produced this mile-deep lake, the deepest on the continent. Undermined by volcanic eruptions, Mount Mazama, once 12,000 feet high, collapsed 6,000 years ago, leaving this vast caldera to fill with water over the ensuing centuries.

216

OREGON

Portland lies upon the Willamette River at its juncture with the Columbia, where there is a port deep enough for the largest ships — indeed, Portland harbor ranks third in ocean-going shipping on the Pacific coast. Full of parks, the city itself is a beautiful and relaxed metropolis.

The ice-wrapped summit of Mount Bachelor (left) is, at over 9,000 feet in height, one of the taller peaks in Deschutes National Forest. The Bachelor, however, is outshone by the Sisters. Swaddled in cloud and snow, the Three Sisters (above) dominate the Three Sisters Wilderness area in the center of the Cascade Range, and are the most majestic alpine group in the region. All exceeding 10,000 feet in height, they are among the most popular of Oregon's major peaks for mountaineers, the North Sister being the most formidable of the three, the South the favorite climb.

NEVADA

Left: an arid land, its need for irrigation self evident, confronts the blue waters of Lake Mead near Las Vegas (top and above) in the extreme south of the state. Nevada itself is a land of extremes: the seventh largest state, it has the second smallest population, while in winter months the temperature can vary from freezing to 70°F. Here, rising from barren deserts, are snowy mountains patterned with ski resorts, while twenty minutes beyond the sophisticated clamor of the Las Vegas gambling circuit there is nothing but the sound of sagebrush rustling in a blistering wind.

CALIFORNIA

Russet red against a jade green sea, San Francisco's Golden Gate Bridge leads north to Marin County. A pure suspension bridge, this famous structure was built in 1937 and has come to symbolize the elegance of this, the loveliest city on the country's Pacific coast.

This page: downtown San Francisco, an American city with a particularly cosmopolitan atmosphere, built on one of the world's finest natural harbors. San Francisco has been rebuilt seven times, having suffered six devastating fires in two years while the town was still young, plus the horrendous, world-famous earthquake of 1906. After years of constructing buildings that rarely exceeded twenty stories, today the city's skyline boasts some magnificent towers, the most distinctive being the Transamerica Corporation building, whose forty-eight floors and crowning spire rise to a point like an elongated pyramid.

Ripples of rock and sand (below) form the scorched landscapes of Death Valley, where the view from Zabriskie Point of the Panamint Range (left) is of some of the continent's most forbidding terrain. In summer it is incredibly hot – a maximum temperature of 134°F in the shade has been recorded here, the world record being 136°F. The valley received its unhappy name after several goldminers lost their way and died in the salt flats when trying to take a short cut through the area. Bottom: cattle and a tractor are almost lost from view among the severe strips of stubble in a field near Livermore, southwest of Stockton.

CALIFORNIA

CALIFORNIA

Facing page top: serried ranks of yachts adorn San Diego's harbor. This city (facing page bottom), California's second largest, has been an important naval headquarters for many years – indeed, 10,000 military personnel are based here –, while San Diego county is a leading agricultural region. Left: Coronado Bay Bridge, a toll bridge that looms over San Diego Bay to connect the city with the Coronado Peninsula, and (below) surf-washed La Jolla, a suburb of San Diego that is said to have the best surfing beach – known as Wind 'n' Sea Beach – this side of Hawaii. Alongside this supposed frivolity, however, La Jolla is also a recognized center for scientific research.

Left: Highway 1 arcs across Bixby Bridge, some 260 feet above Bixby Creek on the precipitous Big Sur coast south of Carmel. This elegant, single-span, concrete highway bridge is one of the world's highest, and the cliff road it graces one of the country's most spectacular. Above: the J. Paul Getty Museum, which overlooks the Pacific Ocean, on the Getty estate in Malibu. Designed as a replica of a first-century Roman villa, a suitable setting for Getty's personal collection of Greek and Roman antiquities, the museum also houses a library of 12,000 volumes and three conservation laboratories. Upon the billionaire's death, just after the collection opened to the public in the mid Seventies, the J. Paul Getty Museum acquired the largest endowment received by any art museum in the world – predictably, perhaps, since Getty was considered to be the richest man on earth at the time of his demise.

CALIFORNIA

A barge floats down the Sacramento Canal between fields of deep green and gold in the Sacramento Valley. Agriculture is fundamental to the Californian economy, and the bulk of it is concentrated in the vast Sacramento Valley, an amazingly fertile, 150-mile-long stretch of farmland watered by the Sacramento River. Sacramento itself has been California's state capital since 1854.

Four years before this, the town had become the western terminal of the Pony Express and later, as the entrance to goldrush country, grew from a population of 6,000 to 10,000 in seven months. Despite suffering seemingly devastating fires and floods during its history, Sacramento has gone from strength to strength.

Above: dotted like toy trees in a child's simple landscape, firs effect a gradual reclamation of the lava beds of Painted Dunes, in Lassen Volcanic National Park. This park, lying in the southernmost part of the Cascade Range, was created to preserve Lassen Peak, a volcano whose eruptions between 1914 and 1921 were responsible for this lava bed. Left: the view from Chimney Rock, in Point Reyes National Seashore. This peninsula is divided from the rest of the state by the main fissure line of the great San Andreas Fault, which is moving the peninsula north at the rate of two inches a year. The epicenter of the 1906 earthquake that destroyed San Francisco, just to the south of this area, was located within Point Reyes – visitors can see where the tremor moved one fence fifteen feet.

The darkened face of Half Dome rears over the Yosemite Valley, in Yosemite National Park, probably America's most famous park. This stunning valley, Yosemite's centerpiece, is just eight miles long, a mile wide and hung with high and powerful waterfalls, among them the highest in North America, Yosemite Falls, which drop a sheer 2,425 feet.

HAWAII

Honolulu Harbor, Oahu, once dominated by the now comparatively diminutive, white Aloha Tower, and today overlooked by the skyscrapers of the city's financial sector. The harbor was discovered in 1800, and in less than 200 years this area has moved from total anonymity to being the nerve center of the state. Honolulu, the Hawaiian capital, contains half the population of Oahu, which, though it is only the third largest island in this six-island archipelago, is home to three-fourths of Hawaii's people. Only a few miles up the coast from the capital lies Pearl Harbor, the seemingly safe refuge where the U.S. naval fleet was destroyed by the Japanese in 1941; the battleships Utah and Arizona still remain here beneath the waves, memorials to the naval personnel who died on that December day.

HAWAII

Waikiki, the Oahu resort that was once a
swamp. The beach is the center of the
city's life: water temperatures are in the
seventies and waves break far out, giving
surfers a fine ride, while swimmers are
protected from strong currents by an
offshore reef – in all, Waikiki Beach is
perfection!

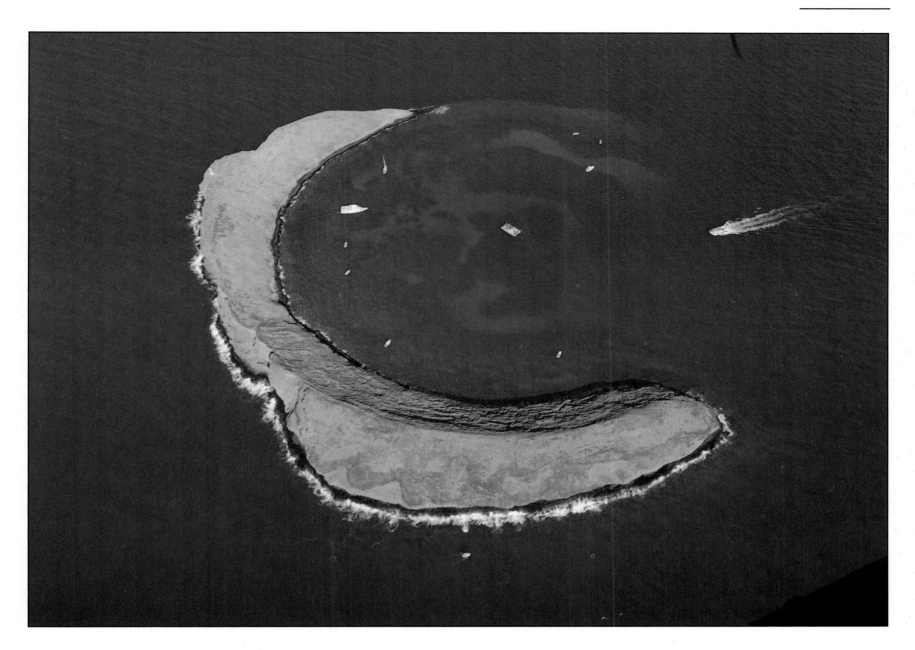

Above: pleasure boats dot the deep blue waters around the surf-fringed crescent of rock known as Molokini, the vestige of a volcano's cone, which lies off the western shores of Maui. The tiny island is primarily known for the fine snorkeling its waters afford, although some Hawaiians continue to consider it the home of their ancestral spirits. Left: the sheer, tree-swathed cliffs to be seen from the ninety-mile-long Hamakua Coast Drive on northeast Hawaii, one of the most scenic drives on the island.

HAWAII

Right: spectacular Na Pali Coast State Park in northwest Kauai, where, forbidding and splendid, the cliffs rise some 2,000 to 3,000 feet above the sea. Until the use of helicopters, these valleys were accessible only from the water – providing the sea was calm! – and as a result they remain uninhabited, though the island of Kauai is believed to have been the first of the six islands to be settled. Above: a sliver-thin stream slices through the tropical cliffs of the Koolau Mountains in eastern Oahu. Rock faces that once streamed with lava are now rich in jungle vegetation – the Koolau range itself is a remnant of the huge volcanoes that formed Oahu.

HAWAII

*Water falls like a lifeline down a cliff as
enclosed and sheer as a mine shaft in
Hona Kane Valley, north Hawaii.*